The Conversation

How to Get Married . . . the Right Way!

by Tony Haygood

The Conversation
How To Get Married…The Right Way
ISBN: 979-8-9881994-0-3
© 2023 by Tony Haygood

Text Design: Lisa Simpson

Dedication

To my lovely wife, Miriam.

Your grace and composure have helped so many, especially me.

Acknowledgments

Writing this curriculum was harder than I thought and more rewarding than I imagined. Still, none of this would have been possible without the help and encouragement of others.

Mark Carrillo, thank you for your unwavering friendship for so many years. You have been an inspiration and a constant source of encouragement to me throughout this project. You possessed the ability to see the potential within me and find a way to bring it forward. I will forever be grateful that you kept me moving, and undoubtedly shaped the course of this entire book. This is only the beginning!

Renae Cockroft, I am so thankful for your tremendous help in editing this book. Your tireless efforts have helped me tremendously, and your valuable suggestions have taken this work to new heights. Thank you for your exceptional talents and relentless commitment. I am so honored that you took on the task of trying to make me sound better!

Lisa Simpson, thank you so much for taking my crazy ideas, thoughts, and run-on sentences, and turning them into something beautiful and readable! Not only are you brilliant and talented, but you are truly a gift!

To my eldest son, Joshua Haygood, thank you for taking the time to capture such amazing images for this book and other projects. You are an extremely talented and creative photographer, having far surpassed anything I ever attempted to do myself. The baton has clearly been passed!

To my daughter-in-law, Megan, and my son-in-law, Will, thank you each for your artistic abilities and creativity. I don't seem to have these skills, but somehow you were able to take the ideas in my brain and turn them into reality for this book. Thank you for bearing with me as it all came together.

To my family and friends, who have endured my unending questions and explanations for so many years, . . . thank you! Your patience allowed me to get it out of my system, and onto the page.

And finally, to my wife, Miriam. Thank you for walking by my side and maintaining a positive attitude, even when I didn't. You have inspired me! You are more patient than me. You are more kind. You are more understanding and balanced. Not only do I love you, but I need you in my life every day. You walk in more wisdom than anyone realizes, especially me. You are an amazing woman! You are beautiful and graceful, and you walk in dignity everywhere you go. I love you so much!

Table of Contents

Foreword

Tony and his wife Miriam have an exemplary marriage and a great family. We attended Bible school and worked together at the church where he served for almost 35 years. Tony was a vital part of the ministry to married couples we helped pioneer there.

Then, as now, Tony is full of the Word and has the ability to communicate biblical truth in a clear, understandable way. He is armed with ample personal experience helping people navigate pre-marital and marriage counseling, through what he calls The Conversation. That conversation is filled with sound scriptural answers and even more thought-provoking questions that will impact your relationships for a lifetime.

It probably goes without saying that the person you marry will have a great impact on your life. Making sure that your relationship is the best that it can be will be a blessing. This book will assist you in having the conversations that will set you up for success in your marriage. The fact that you picked up this book tells me that you are interested in having the conversations that will help make that possible.

Mark Carrillo

Author's Note

WHY I WROTE THIS BOOK

Welcome to The Conversation! My name is Tony Haygood, and my wife and I have been married since 1989. We have seven beautiful children and many grandchildren. Having worked in and around Christian Ministry since the mid-1980s, I have aided many couples in starting and building successful marriages. But unfortunately, I have seen many endure the difficulties of separation and divorce. That inspired me to write this book. The information in this workbook will provide you with the necessary tools and knowledge to start the extraordinary journey of marriage.

I have chosen to use the word "conversation" rather than "counseling" throughout this book to create a comfortable and relaxed atmosphere.

The things we will discuss are intended to make you think about your future together—your life, family, and marriage. Knowing why you believe what you believe and establishing a durable foundation for your life together is essential. I will ask you questions, share some Bible scriptures, and encourage you along the way. This is so crucial for the success of your life together. Please be forthright in your responses and thoughts. My role is to guide you, helping you be as prepared as possible for your life together.

To show you "How to get Married . . . The Right Way!"

Tony Haygood

How To Use This Curriculum

Whether you are a minister counseling a couple before marriage or a couple considering marriage, this book is for you! The pages are meant to be eye-opening and thought-provoking. The idea here is not to attempt to talk you into or out of the marriage but to prompt you to seriously consider your future lives together and the many facets involved. Information can be valuable, and understanding and applying that information can be priceless!

Please take your time and review each of these chapters. Consider the information carefully and how it will affect and challenge you to be the best version of yourself. Your future spouse deserves that. It is best to start at the beginning and work your way through to the end, taking in all the information presented, one piece at a time. You will see that each chapter will bring out additional thoughts that build on the last.

Taking your time and not rushing through the material is also helpful. It would be best to allow plenty of time to complete the course long before your wedding date. You need to comprehend what is being taught and the questions being asked. Limiting yourselves to an hour and a half per session is usually better to ensure your attention and comprehension levels remain high. At this pace, you can expect to cover several chapters in one sitting and complete everything in five or six sessions. This, of course, depends on how long you need to discuss individual questions and address any of your questions that may arise along the way. If you are a minister using this material, you should consider approximately six sessions for completion.

Well, that is about it! I am excited for you to begin, and I know that the beautiful journey of marriage will be more enriching because you cared enough to take the time to prepare!

Questions to Consider Before Marriage

Let us begin by considering some basic questions about your relationship. Take time to think about what you are doing and why you are doing it. Your answers will help you gauge whether you are ready for marriage.

1. How do you know that you are truly in love?

_____

_____

2. What are your reasons for wanting to get married?

_____

_____

3. What activities do you enjoy doing together?

_____

_____

4. In one word, how would you describe your partner?

_____

_____

5. Have either of you been deeply in love before?

_____

_____

6. Why did you decide to read this book?

_____

_____

7. Can you see yourself being married for the rest of your life?

_____

_____

8. What does the term "Christian marriage" mean to you?

_____

_____

9. How is a Christian marriage different from other marriages?

_____

_____

10. Why do you believe your marriage will be successful?

_____

_____

11. How do your friends and family feel about your relationship?

_____

_____

12. Do you feel that you are sacrificing anything significant to be in this relationship?

_____

_____

13. Do you have any major concerns about getting married?

_____

_____

14. Have either of you been married before?

_____

_____

15. How long has it been since the last time you fell deeply in love?

_____

_____

16. How is your current relationship different from past relationships?

_____

_____

17. What is the spiritual aspect of your relationship?

_____

_____

18. What are some of your partner's strengths?

_____

_____

19. What about your partner attracted you to them?

_____

_____

20. Do you discuss your faith with each other?

_____

_____

21. Are you able to be honest and open with each other?

_____

_____

22. Have you ever viewed pornography, or are you currently?

_____

_____

23. Do you believe that the love you have can develop into a more mature, committed love?

_____

_____

24. Are you willing to confront any potential red flags that may arise while reading this book?

_____

_____

Answering those questions will enable you to open yourself and honestly approach all the topics throughout this curriculum.

1

The Covenant of Marriage

Introduction:

Have you ever really thought about what real commitment means? In the context of marriage, it should be one of the first and most important considerations. The commitment to marriage is not something to be taken lightly. It is not a temporary arrangement that easily can be ended if things do not go as planned. Instead, marriage is a **sacred, lifetime covenant** between one man and one woman. It is a public vow that defines how you will interact with each other to form a new family unit. It is a serious, meaningful, and sacred union. It is sacred because God has set it apart and blessed it.

Instruction:

It is important to note that marriage is not just a contract but a **covenant.** *There is an enormous difference!*

A contract has these essential characteristics:

1. Contracts are most often made for a limited period.

2. Contracts often deal with very specific things.

3. Contracts are based on conditions being met.

4. Contracts are motivated by the desire to get something.

A covenant has these essential characteristics:

1. Covenants are initiated for the benefit of the other person.

2. Covenant relationships are based on steadfast love.

3. Covenant relationships view commitments as permanent.

4. Covenants are based on unconditional promises.

A marriage covenant is a sacred bond made before God and other witnesses. It is a promise to love, honor, and cherish each other through sickness and health, for better or worse, until death do us part. A marriage covenant is a lifelong commitment based on trust, faith, and the belief that God brought you together for a divine purpose.

One of the primary differences between a marriage contract and a marriage covenant is their focus. A marriage contract is primarily concerned with the legal and financial aspects of the relationship, whereas a marriage covenant is centered on the spiritual and emotional connection between the couple. In addition, while a marriage contract is enforceable by law, a marriage covenant is upheld by the couple's commitment to each other and their faith in God.

A covenant surpasses the duration of a contract!

While a contract defines that "if you do this, then I will do that," a covenant states, "I will do this, until death do us part." If one of the parties fails to fulfill a contract, the entire agreement becomes null and void, and both parties are free to walk away. Contract signers agree to honor their part of the deal only if the other signer holds up theirs.

Conversely, in a covenant, both parties agree to uphold their part of the agreement regardless of the other party's actions. Even if one party violates the covenant, the other party remains committed to fulfilling their end of the deal. A covenant involves both parties continuing with their responsibility to fulfill their promises, regardless of the other's performance. Furthermore, not only is a covenant perpetual, but it is also irrevocable! **It is important that you have a clear understanding that your marriage covenant is forever.**

A marriage covenant includes a guarantee, but it is not the type of guarantee you might expect. The guarantee is on the individual's part, not their spouse's. It is a pledge you make to your spouse, promising to uphold **your** commitment, not theirs. Again, a true Bible-based marriage is rightly seen as a covenant between one man, one woman, and God Himself.

Now, almost everyone is familiar with the two little words that are said by nearly everyone who decides to get married. Those simple words most often stated at the altar — "I Do." But did you ever stop to think how important those two little words are? Those two little words say quite a bit about the entire future of your marriage. Because when you say, "I Do," you are not saying "I Did," or even "I Will." That little word "Do" is a now word! It is an active word, a progressive word, a continuous word, a repetitive word, and a present tense word!

You have probably often heard that "Little words control great destinies." Well, that "I Do" will control the direction and destiny of your whole marriage. It is essential to make sure you understand what "I Do" means and to make sure you understand what you are agreeing to when you say, "I Do." If you do not pay attention here, you could end up with an "I Do" problem. Remember, it is "I Do," not "I Did!" "I Did," says it is over. "I Will," says it is not here yet. You must keep saying "I Do" after you say it the first time!

So, how exactly do you continue to say, "I Do?" Well, after you say "I Do" when you get married, you can continue to keep your love alive by doing some of the following things:

- Talking and touching a lot. I mean a lot! If you spend more time talking to and touching your mobile phone than your spouse, you might want to look closer at your marriage priorities!

- You can also help one another with things that mean a lot to them. This is an unselfish way to demonstrate your love for each other.

- Support one another and be ready to back each other up.

- It is also essential to watch your words to your partner. Words can hurt or heal. So, watch what you say and how you say it.

- Just being there for one another is enormous! Make sure they know they can always count on you.

- Submit to one another. Strongly desire to help each other.

- Completely trust your spouse.

- Completely believe the best of your spouse.

Questions to Consider:

1. Are you ready to permanently commit yourself to this marriage?

_____

_____

2 Do you really understand this is for the rest of your life?

_____

_____

3. Do you understand that you must maintain your marriage for it to be successful?

_____

_____

4. Will you agree to completely hold up your end of the deal, even if your spouse does not?

_____

_____

5. Do you understand the importance of watching your words?

_____

_____

6. What two little words must you keep in front of you throughout your marriage?

_____

_____

Summary:

Marriage is all about a lifelong commitment to one another! The covenant of marriage is never-ending. As husband and wife, it is your job to continue to choose to love each other, no matter what comes your way. One of the ways to keep your love and marriage alive is to continue to do the things you know will bless your spouse daily.

Notes:

_____

_____

_____

2

Mutual Expectations and Goals

When two individuals decide to marry, they bring their unique expectations about the relationship, roles, and future together. Individual experiences, cultural backgrounds, and personal values often shape these expectations. Considering mutual expectations when getting married is essential because unmet expectations can lead to dissatisfaction and conflict. When couples have different expectations about important aspects of marriage, such as communication, intimacy, financial management, and parenting, it can create tension and misunderstandings, causing stress and strain on the relationship. Discussing and aligning your expectations beforehand can establish a strong foundation for your marriage, build mutual trust and understanding, and develop strategies to address potential conflicts.

Additionally, considering mutual expectations can help you understand each other better and make informed decisions about your future together. By having open and honest conversations about your expectations, you can gain insight into each other's priorities and goals, facilitating better decision-making about essential matters, such as career choices, living arrangements, and starting a family. It can also help you anticipate and prepare for potential challenges, such as health or financial status changes, which can impact your expectations and require adjustments in your relationship. Finally, mutual expectations are crucial for a successful marriage, fostering understanding, respect, and commitment to each other's needs and desires.

Instruction:

God assigned distinct and differing roles to man and woman at creation. However, they were both created in God's image; therefore, their roles were equal in value but different in function. These roles were assigned **before** the fall of man in the Garden of Eden. The pattern of biblical roles within marriage continued throughout the Old Testament. In the New Testament, the roles of husband and wife symbolize Christ and His church. Christian men are to lay down their lives for their wives lovingly. They still maintain leadership, but this must be servant leadership. Husbands are not to demand obedience but to guide through humility. Men are to honor their wives and to lead and lovingly serve them.

The Bible exalts womanhood in the home and places great value on it. Women are to follow their husband's leadership respectfully, choosing to submit to that leadership. The Bible states that when wives submit to their husbands' leadership, they do it to serve God. A woman can be a great blessing and help to her husband. A woman's priority is her husband, family, and home life.

Men and women were created with distinct abilities to fulfill these biblical roles, and when husbands and wives follow the biblical pattern within the home, they bring glory to God as a picture of Christ and His church.

Here are several scriptural principles which are essential for a strong marriage:

1. Love — The Bible commands husbands to love their wives and wives to respect their husbands (Ephesians 5:33). Love is an essential ingredient for a strong marriage, as it involves selflessness, sacrificial service, and unconditional acceptance.

2. Forgiveness — No marriage is perfect, and conflicts are bound to arise. However, the Bible teaches us to forgive each other as Christ forgave us (Colossians 3:13). Forgiveness is essential for a healthy, lasting marriage, allowing couples to move past hurts and conflicts and restore their relationship.

3. Communication — Effective communication is essential for building and maintaining a solid marriage. The Bible instructs us to be slow to speak, quick to listen, and slow to anger (James 1:19). By listening to each other, expressing thoughts and feelings, and resolving conflicts respectfully and lovingly, couples can strengthen their relationship and deepen their intimacy.

4. Unity — The Bible teaches that a husband and wife are no longer two but one flesh (Matthew 19:6). This unity is essential. It involves shared values, goals, and priorities. As a result, couples can strengthen their bond and build a lasting relationship by working together, supporting each other, and putting their marriage first.

5. Trust — Trust is a vital component of a strong marriage. The Bible instructs us to be trustworthy, honest, and faithful in our relationships (Proverbs 20:6). By being transparent, reliable, and accountable, couples can build trust and deepen their intimacy.

A lasting marriage requires love, forgiveness, communication, unity, and trust. All these things are rooted in biblical principles. Applying these principles to your relationship can build a lasting marriage that honors God and fulfills your deepest desires.

Questions to Consider:

1. Do either of you have unaddressed addictions or significant emotional baggage from your past?

   _____

   _____

2. What level of emotional support do you expect from your partner during times of excitement, depression, illness, and job loss?

   _____

   _____

3. Do you believe it is essential to set aside regular alone time for the two of you to catch up and have fun?

   _____

   _____

4. Do both of you communicate the amount of alone time that you each need?

   _____

   _____

5. How much time should you spend with friends individually and together?

   _____

   _____

6. Have you agreed on how much time is appropriate to devote to work? This can be a critical issue for many individuals.

   _____

   _____

7. Do you both plan to support the family financially, and if so, will that change when you have children?

_____

_____

8. Are you both comfortable with the salary differences between each other?

_____

_____

9. What are your career aspirations for the future?

_____

_____

10. Are you okay with living with things about each other that may bother you for the rest of your life?

_____

_____

11. Who will be responsible for various household tasks such as cleaning dishes, laundry, ironing, vacuuming, taking out the trash, cleaning bathrooms, lawn maintenance, home repairs, finances, and meal preparation?

_____

_____

12. Regarding household chores, do either of you have personal preferences that could help determine who will do which tasks?

_____

_____

13. If neither of you wants to perform a particular household or yard maintenance task, how do you plan to handle it?

_____

_____

Summary:

Marriage brings together two individuals and entirely different people. If you can take the time to understand those differences, you can avoid some of life's pitfalls. It is vital to keep your communication lines open and be honest with each other along the way. Together, you can work to resolve differences and have a thriving marriage!

Notes:

_____

_____

_____

_____

_____

_____

_____

_____

_____

_____

3

Living Arrangements

One of the most important decisions you will make when getting married is choosing a living arrangement and place that works for both of you. The most important thing when choosing a living arrangement is to communicate openly and honestly with each other. Discuss your preferences and concerns, and work together to find a solution for both of you.

There are several factors to consider when making this decision, including:

- Budget: You must ensure that your living arrangement is affordable and will not put undue financial strain on your new household.

- Location: You and your partner should discuss your preferences and needs regarding proximity to work, family, and other key factors.

- Space: The size of your living space is also essential. You will want to ensure enough room for both of you to live comfortably, including adequate storage space for your belongings.

- Homeownership: If you plan to buy a home, you must ensure that you are both comfortable with the financial commitment and responsibilities of homeownership. You may also need to consider other factors, such as property maintenance and renovations.

- Family considerations: If you have or plan to have children, you must ensure that your living arrangement suits them. You may need to consider factors such as school districts and proximity to family-friendly amenities.

- Lifestyle considerations: Your lifestyle preferences and needs should also be considered when choosing a living arrangement. For example, if you enjoy hosting parties, you must ensure that your living space can accommodate your guests.

Instruction:

If I were to ask you to describe your house, you might mention its beautiful front door, the size, the number of stories, and whether it has a brick or wooden exterior. You might also talk about its location and the flower garden at the entryway. However, it is unlikely that you would mention how solid its foundation or level it is. For example, you would not describe how the footers were dug, how the plumbing pipes were laid in the ground, or how great the electrical conduit was that came through the concrete foundation. But without a solid foundation, the other features would not work properly.

Ephesians 4:14-16 "So that we may no longer be children, tossed to and fro by the waves and carried about by every wind of doctrine, by human cunning, by craftiness in deceitful schemes. Rather, speaking the truth in love, we are to grow up in every way into him who is the head, into Christ, from whom the whole body, joined and held together by every joint with which it is equipped, when each part is working properly, makes the body grow so that it builds itself up in love."

If you compare the body of Christ or your marriage to a brick building, you will see that the bricks would topple over if they were not joined together. This is because the concrete mortar between those bricks forms those bricks into a solid wall held in place by the effectual working of every other brick. Yet even a solid brick wall is only of value if it sits on a solid foundation.

A foundation is one of the most important things you will never see!

Always remember the significance of a sturdy foundation, whether in building a structure or establishing a marriage. Vast sums of money and considerable efforts go into unseen groundwork like concrete, large pipes, cables, and footers. If you are tempted to skimp on the foundation, a wise architect will remind you that "nothing is more important than the foundation."

CONSIDER THESE FIVE POINTS ABOUT FOUNDATIONS AND MARRIAGE:

1. A good foundation is crucial for the strength of any building, and the same goes for your marriage.

2. With a solid foundation, both a building and a marriage can withstand stress and pressure.

3. The strength of a building is directly proportional to the quality of its foundation, just as the strength of a marriage is linked to the quality of its foundation.

4. The higher you want your marriage to go, the more critical it is to have a sturdy foundation.

5. A great building's foundation is not immediately visible, and the same is true of a strong marriage's foundation, but it is essential for your marriage's growth, strength, and quality.

Also, consider the following:

• Foundations, like trees, are stationary and do not move. Have you ever seen a strong five or 6-story mobile home? There is a reason for that.

- House foundations comprise many key ingredients to ensure good strength. The elements that strengthen your marriage foundation are righteousness, purity, holiness, prayer, commitment, faithfulness, obedience, and trust.

- Establishing individual godly foundations is crucial to building a strong marriage foundation, which helps establish a family foundation. This leads to a Church Foundation, where each foundation is a stepping stone to the next.

- Be aware that many things will challenge the foundation of your life - beliefs, faith, family, friends, health, and finances. Psalm 11:3 states, "If the foundations are destroyed, what can the righteous do?" Therefore, be prepared for your foundation to be tested.

Despite these challenges, there are several principles you can follow to build a solid marriage foundation.

COMMITMENT

Committing to anything has become less popular in our society, where individual rights, personal freedom, and mobility are emphasized. However, building a strong, divorce-proof marriage requires giving up some selfish personal rights. It means your commitment to the relationship supersedes your rights while maintaining some freedom and choices. Commitment means putting your spouse's needs above your own and finding satisfaction in consistently meeting them.

COMMUNICATION

Communication is the lifeblood of a marriage. It involves sharing feelings, hurts, and joys, not just exchanging information. Men and women differ in this area, with research showing that women have greater linguistic abilities than men. To maintain a healthy relationship, husbands must learn to communicate their feelings better. The inability or unwillingness of husbands to reveal their emotions is often a complaint of wives. Communication is a learned skill and requires effort and hard work.

PATIENCE

We live in a fast-paced world where everything is instant - Solid State Hard Drives, ATMs, Smartphones, Bill Pay, microwave popcorn. . . you name it! However, marriage is not something that can be rushed or micro-waved. It takes time, care, and patience to develop an excellent relationship. When you put two people in the same house, irritations and annoyances are inevitable, but patience is essential for the long haul. It may take years to build a satisfying relationship, but the wait is worth it.

STRONG BELIEFS

Research shows that couples with strong religious beliefs are more likely to stay together than those without them. Shared morals and values hold a husband and wife together and provide a fortress against the storms of life. Jesus spoke about two different foundations for life, which are equally applicable to a couple building a home and marriage together.

Matthew 7:24–27 "Everyone then who hears these words of mine and does them will be like a wise man who built his house on the rock. And the rain fell, and the floods came, and the winds blew and beat on that house, but it did not fall, because it had been founded on the rock. And everyone who hears these words of mine and does not do them will be like a foolish man who built his house on the sand. And the rain fell, and the floods came, and the winds blew and beat against that house, and it fell, and great was the fall of it."

Questions to Consider:

1. Will you live in a house or apartment? Consider the pros and cons of each and what best fits your lifestyle and budget.

_____

_____

2. Will you rent or purchase your living space? Think about your financial situation and long-term goals.

_____

_____

3. If you plan to have children, where will you live after they arrive? Consider the space and location needed for a growing family.

_____

_____

4. How will you determine if a new career path or job is reason enough to move? Discuss your priorities and options for relocating.

_____

_____

5. Do you hope to live in the same house or area for a long time, or will you change often? Consider your future goals and preferences.

_____

_____

6. Do either of you have a certain house in mind that you would consider a dream home? Discuss your ideal living situation and see if it aligns with your budget and priorities.

_____

_____

7. Will you need to be close to your parents now or as they age? Consider the potential need for support and assistance from family members.

_____

_____

8. Will the distance from home to church keep you from attending regularly? Think about your commitment to your faith and prioritize attending worship services.

_____

_____

9. Do either of you specifically desire a one or two-story home? How important is it to have a large yard?

_____

_____

10. If work conditions change, are you willing to move to accommodate? Discuss the possibility of relocation and how it fits your career and life goals.

_____

_____

Summary:

How and where you will live is important to discuss, but not nearly as important as the foundation on which a marriage will be built! Taking time at the beginning of your marriage is crucial to ensure your foundation is situated correctly and ready to go the distance. It is up to you to pay close attention to your commitment to one another, your communication, and the patience you display toward one another. These things all work together to create a solid and lasting marriage.

Notes:

_____

_____

4

Conflict & Communication

Happy couples have realistic expectations. One myth is that healthy couples do not even have conflicts. But conflict is inevitable. Any time you take two different, independent people with diverse backgrounds and upbringings, who have different tastes in food, movies, and recreational activities, different ideas about decorating, landscaping, vehicles, time, and money... and suddenly put them in a position to live together in the same place... and add a couple of pets, you have the potential for relationship conflict! Be on your guard!

Instruction:

In any marriage, there are bound to be challenges and obstacles that couples must navigate together. These challenges include constant fighting, miscommunication, household chores, jealousy, keeping secrets, and not getting along with your spouse's family. However, as Christians, it is essential to approach these challenges with love, grace, and a biblical perspective.

Constant fighting can damage a marriage by creating a toxic environment where neither partner feels heard nor understood. The Bible tells us to *"let all bitterness and wrath and anger and clamor and slander be put away from you, along with all malice"* (Ephesians 4:31). Instead, we should strive to communicate with gentleness and respect, seeking to understand each other's perspective.

Miscommunication can lead to misunderstandings and hurt feelings. As Christians, we are called to *"speak the truth in love"* (Ephesians 4:15). This means being honest with each other and compassionate and understanding. We should also strive to listen actively and empathetically to understand our spouse's thoughts and feelings.

Household chores can be a source of tension in a marriage, particularly if one partner feels that they are doing more than their fair share. However, the Bible tells us to *"Do nothing from selfish ambition or conceit, but in humility count others more significant than yourselves"* (Philippians 2:3). This means being willing to serve each other and putting our partner's needs ahead of our own.

Jealousy can be a destructive force in marriage, leading to feelings of insecurity and mistrust. The Bible warns us against envy and jealousy, saying, *"Let us not become conceited, provoking one another, envying one another"* (Galatians 5:26). Instead, we should trust in God's plan for our lives and strive to build each other up rather than tearing each other down.

Keeping secrets can erode trust in a marriage, creating a sense of distance and isolation. Instead, the Bible tells us to *"walk in the light, as he is in the light, we have fellowship with one another"* (1 John 1:7). This means being honest and transparent with each other, even if it means admitting our faults or mistakes.

Not having a good relationship with your spouse's family can create tension and division in marriage. As Christians, we are called to *"honor your father and mother"* (Ephesians 6:2). This means being respectful and kind to our spouse's family, even if we do not always see eye-to-eye.

Sometimes you also just need some space. This is a relatively easy thing to do. It is just a simple decision away. Just because you can legally shower together all the time does not mean you should. Regarding privacy, keep your love and sex life off all social media! It is ok to say that you love your spouse, but nobody needs to ever know the details of what goes on behind your closed doors. Nobody!

So, you need to give freedom to your spouse to have friends, love others, talk to others, and have fun with others, knowing and trusting them to do the same.

The other side to this is something to watch for: It is when the pendulum swings too far in the other direction. When you begin to enjoy that freedom to the point that you want to stay away from your spouse or stay away from home. So many married Christians are just tolerating each other. They do not want to get divorced because they know enough about God's Word, and they honestly believe that is wrong, but they do not even like to be together. Most of the time, this is a direct result of miscommunication or an ungodly outside influence, both of which can be fixed!

Questions to Consider:

1. Do you or your partner have a problem handling anger?

_____

_____

2. Do you have trouble trusting your partner?

_____

_____

3. How well do you handle conflict as a couple?

_____

_____

4. When you have conflict, do you fight fairly?

   _____

   _____

5. How did your parents settle their differences?

   _____

   _____

6. What are the customs that may affect what you expect in terms of expressed anger?

   _____

   _____

7. During a conflict, a person either yields, withdrawals, compromises, wins, or resolves. Which of these tends to be your style? Which of these tends to be your partner's style?

   _____

   _____

8. How will you handle it when your partner gets upset?

   _____

   _____

9. Can either of you ask for a time-out to calm down and be creative in your problem-solving?

   _____

   _____

10. Do either of you struggle with apologizing or owning your mistakes? How can you grow in this area?

    _____

    _____

11. How will you make decisions together?

_____

_____

12. Are you both willing to face difficult situations, or do you try to avoid conflict altogether?

_____

_____

13. Do you attempt to sweep things under the rug and delay resolution?

_____

_____

14. Do you think you have problems in your relationship that you need to deal with before your wedding?

_____

_____

15. Do you think you handle conflict well?

_____

_____

16. Do you think your differences will create problems in your marriage?

_____

_____

17. Do you expect or want each other to change?

_____

_____

18. Can you both forgive one another?

_____

_____

19. Are you both willing to work on your communication skills?

_____

_____

20. What steps will you take to give one another healthy personal space or alone time?

_____

_____

21. Can you both deal with constructive criticism?

_____

_____

22. Do you or your partner constantly complain?

_____

_____

23. Do you find yourself arguing a lot with your partner?

_____

_____

24. Do you refrain from giving your opinion or true thoughts because of fear of your partner's reaction?

_____

_____

25. Are you or your partner secretive or do you suspect your partner hides things from you?

_____

_____

Summary:

A healthy and thriving marriage requires patience, grace, and a commitment to following God's plan. By approaching challenges with a biblical perspective and a spirit of love and forgiveness, you can overcome any obstacle and grow stronger as a couple.

Notes:

_____

_____

_____

_____

_____

_____

_____

_____

_____

_____

_____

_____

5

Intimacy

MEN AND WOMEN ARE DIFFERENT!

Imagine if a new store just opened in town that sells "new husbands." A place where a woman may go to choose a husband. The instructions at the entrance to the store describe how the store operates. A woman may visit the store ONLY ONCE! There are six floors, and the attributes of the men increase as the shopper ascends to each floor. But there is a catch: you may choose any man from a particular floor or decide to go up to look for someone better, but you cannot go back down except to exit the building.

So, a woman goes to the Husband Store to find a husband, and on the first floor, the sign on the door reads, Floor 1 — These men have jobs. "Great!" thinks the woman, "but I wonder what else is here?" She ascends to the second floor, where the sign reads: Floor 2 — These men have jobs and love kids. "Oh!" "Even better!" she exclaims. The third-floor sign reads Floor 3 — These men have jobs, love kids, and are extremely good-looking. "Wow," she thinks but feels compelled to keep going. She goes to the fourth floor, where the sign reads: Floor 4 — These men have jobs, love kids, are drop-dead good-looking, and help with all the housework. "Oh," she says, "I can hardly stand it!" Still, she goes to the fifth floor where the sign reads: Floor 5 — These men have jobs, love kids, are drop-dead gorgeous, help with the housework, and have a strong romantic streak. She is so tempted to stay, but she goes to the sixth floor where the sign reads: Floor 6 — You are visitor 31,456,012 to this floor. There are no men on this floor. This floor exists solely as proof that women are impossible to please. Thank you for shopping at the Husband Store. Please exit the building.

Ironically, a "new wives" store with the same basic rules recently opened across the street. The first-floor sign reads Floor 1 — These wives love sex. The second through sixth floors have never been visited. This shows how different men and women are!

Instruction:

Paul addressed the topic of sexual intimacy in his first letter to the Corinthian church.

I Corinthians 7:2–5 "But because of the temptation to sexual immorality, each man should have his own wife and each woman her own husband. The husband should give his wife her conjugal rights, and likewise the wife to her husband. The wife does not have authority over her own body, but the husband does. Likewise, the husband does not have authority over his own body, but the wife does. Do not deprive one another, except perhaps by agreement for a limited time, that you may devote yourselves to prayer; but then come together again, so that Satan may not tempt you because of your lack of self-control."

Paul understood that unmet sexual needs and desires within the marriage covenant are dangerous. When men and women do not meet their partner's needs, it gives Satan a powerful foothold for temptation. This is true with all marital needs but especially regarding sex.

LISTEN UP, BRIDE:

If you lined up a hundred men in a room and asked them one at a time to tell you what they need and desire most from their wives, two surprising things would happen.

First, every one of them would be able to answer that question.

Second, their answers would be very, very similar.

Most men have four basic needs that they want to be met by a marriage partner.

1. They need to feel honored and respected by their wives.

2. They need sexual intimacy.

3. They need friendship - a wife who enjoys doing fun things together.

4. They need domestic support - a wife caring for the home.

Men have a profound physical and emotional need for sex. And women have been given the gift of sex. So when women withhold that gift from their husbands, it creates a breeding ground for sexual sin and temptation.

Men do not just desire sex from their wives. They need it to feel whole and complete as marriage partners. Therefore, when we enter the marriage covenant, we surrender the rights to our own body to our partner. In Paul's words, "The wife does not have authority over her own body but yields it to her husband. In the same way, the husband does not have authority over his own body but yields it to his wife."

Nowhere else in Scripture are we given a more graphic example of what it means to become one flesh. In marriage, we willingly grant our partners complete access to everything we have, including our bodies. It is the ultimate act of service and humility.

LISTEN UP, GROOM:

Just as a man needs a wife who will tend to his basic needs and desires, a woman needs a husband who cares about her needs and makes it his job to fulfill them. What she most needs from him can also be summed up in four primary categories.

1. Women need security. They need to know that their most basic needs are taken care of and that they are physically, emotionally, and financially secure. They need to feel nurtured, cherished, and loved.

2. Women need affection. They need nonsexual intimacy and care.

3. Women need communication. They need a husband who will open his heart and communicate honestly, without reserve.

4. Women need leadership. They need a husband willing to take charge and guide the family.

Love was designed to grow deeper and stronger with time. To become even more intimate and rewarding. To meet our deepest needs and desires. To not only last but to grow healthier and fuller with age. **If you want to stay in love, you must stay in like!** Your job is to discover and meet your spouse's needs.

Questions to Consider:

1. Have either of you experienced any abuse that has not been addressed?

_____

_____

2. Have you talked openly about your sexual history?

_____

_____

3. Do you get the attention and healthy affection you desire from your partner?

_____

_____

4. How often do you want to enjoy an intimate evening with each other?

_____

_____

5. How do you intend to resolve differences in sexual preferences?

_____

_____

6. Can you agree on how to deal with differences in sexual desire in terms of frequency?

_____

_____

7. During sex, are certain things off-limits to you?

_____

_____

8. Do you agree to discuss your sexual concerns when you both feel creative and relaxed, and not during sex?

_____

_____

9. Have you made any decisions about birth control? What methods will you choose to use? (i.e., birth control pills, condoms, etc.)

_____

_____

10. Do either of you have trust issues or feel insecure?

_____

_____

11. How important is affirmation to you?

_____

_____

Suggestions and tips

- Take your time with sex! It is not a rush. Give plenty of time for foreplay, back rubs, etc. Make it a comfortable, intimate time for both of you. Do not rush it.

- Avoid putting perfume or cologne on or near your intimate areas, as this can burn or irritate your spouse's skin or intimate areas. Also true with oils, lubricants, etc.

- Make sure if you are using condoms that you or your spouse do not have a latex allergy.

- Sex positions: I suggest a book by Sheila Wray Gregoire called "The Good Girls Guide To Great Sex."

- Different sex positions will develop over time, and you must find what works best for both of you. Be open to your partner's desires and communicate a lot about what works and what does not. Some positions can be more painful than others.

- For the Bride – Consider investigating pre-stretching your hymen to help deter some of the pain that can be associated with sex for the first time.

Summary:

Intimacy in marriage is vital to a thriving relationship. It is essential for both of you to know and understand what that means to each other. Intimacy is also something that is built upon and discovered along the way.

Notes:

6

Handling Money

Introduction:

This chapter is longer than most of the others. This is because handling money in marriage has been one of the leading causes of conflict and tension for a long time. It is a topic that is too often avoided or ignored entirely, but couples must have open and honest conversations about their finances. Properly handling money in marriage requires communication, teamwork, and discipline. So, this chapter is longer on purpose! We will begin with instructions on handling money properly from a practical perspective and finish this chapter by discussing what to do if things go wrong.

Instruction:

Let us talk about some practical ways of managing money in marriage from a biblical perspective.

- Communication is vital when it comes to managing money in marriage. Couples should regularly discuss their financial goals, priorities, and challenges. My wife and I have regular meetings about our money. We call these meetings "State of the Union meetings."

We always try to be transparent about our income, expenses, debts, and savings. This helps us to develop a shared vision for our financial future and avoid surprises or misunderstandings. Setting aside time for these discussions and approaching them with a spirit of humility, respect, and understanding is important.

- Teamwork is another important aspect of managing money in marriage. Couples should work together to create a budget that reflects their goals and values. They should allocate their income to different categories such as housing, food, transportation, healthcare, education, entertainment, investments, and savings. They should also track their expenses to ensure they stay within their budget and identify areas where they can reduce their spending. Both partners must contribute to the financial planning and decision-making process, regardless of who earns the most money.

- Discipline is the third component of managing money in marriage. Couples should exercise self-control and avoid impulsive or reckless spending. They should prioritize their needs over their wants and resist the temptation to keep up with others' lifestyles or expectations. They should also avoid debt as much as possible, especially high-interest consumer debt such as credit cards or personal loans. If they have debt, they should develop a plan to pay it off as soon as possible and avoid accumulating more debt.

From a biblical perspective, managing money in marriage involves stewardship, generosity, and faith. Christians believe that God owns everything and that they are simply managers or stewards of His resources. Therefore, they should use money wisely and responsibly to honor God and serve others. They should also be generous and give to those in need, whether within their own family, church, or community. The Bible teaches that generosity is crucial to Christian discipleship. God blesses those who give cheerfully and generously.

In addition, managing money in marriage requires faith in God's provision and wisdom. Couples should trust that God will provide for their needs and guide them in their financial decisions. They should seek His wisdom through prayer, Bible study, and counsel from wise and trustworthy advisors. They should also avoid anxiety, worry, or greed, knowing God cares for them and their true treasure is in heaven.

Here are some practical tips for managing money in marriage from a biblical perspective:

- Set financial goals that are aligned with your values and priorities.

- Create a budget that reflects your income, expenses, and savings.

- Avoid debt as much as possible and develop a plan to pay it off if you have it.

- Be disciplined and avoid impulsive or reckless spending.

- Be generous and give to those in need.

- Trust in God's provision and wisdom.

Properly handling money in marriage is crucial for building a healthy and thriving relationship.

I ALSO WANT TO TALK ABOUT FACING FINANCIAL TROUBLES AND LEARNING TO TRUST GOD WITH YOUR MONEY:

The Bible, taken as a whole, presents a massive cooperative effort on the part of God and man. He has done His part; now, it is up to us to take Him at His Word, trust Him, and cooperate with the Word He has given us.

The question is . . . When you face a financial problem, is it a product of your poor decisions, an attack from the evil one, or a combination of both? It does not matter because financial problems need to be addressed by the truth found in the Word of God, regardless! So, what can you do about your finances? What can you say about it? What can you believe about it? Let us face it . . . Financial troubles are genuine, and they can crush your marriage!

They can cause friction and arguments, bitterness, contention, blame, hopelessness, and even snuff out your future plans. They can ruin your mindset, keep you gloomy, destroy your sex life, steal your time, etc. In other words, financial troubles are horrible! It is high time we directly address your personal and business financial problems, lack, debt, and all the other junk that comes with money problems. We will break the back of lack, delay, and hindrances and see God's best come forth! I will share a few things from the Word of God, and then we will pray over your finances!

So, what is it that makes the difference in your finances? What takes you from where you are to where you want to be? How do you do it?

Psalm 119:130 (KJV) "The entrance of thy words giveth light; it giveth understanding unto the simple."

Psalm 73:17 "Until I went into the sanctuary of God; then understood I their end."

Take a deep breath. Relax, and understand that God wants the absolute best for you, even more than you want it for you. In 3 John 2 (KJV), John wrote, *"Beloved, I wish above all things that thou mayest prosper and be in health, even as thy soul prospereth."* But the same Bible that brought us also brought us 2 Thessalonians 3:10 (KJV), *"For even when we were with you, this we commanded you, that if any would not work, neither should he eat."*

All through the Bible, God put giving first! Therefore, you cannot talk about finances and increase without talking about giving.

Galatians 2:20 "I have been crucified with Christ. It is no longer I who live, but Christ who lives in me. And the life I now live in the flesh I live by faith in the Son of God, who loved me and gave himself for me."

Luke 6:38 "Give, and it will be given to you. Good measure, pressed down, shaken together, running over, will be put into your lap. For with the measure, you use it will be measured back to you."

John 3:16 "For God so loved the world, that he gave his only Son, that whoever believes in him should not perish but have eternal life."

Deuteronomy 15:7 "If among you, one of your brothers should become poor, in any of your towns within your land that the LORD your God is giving you, you shall not harden your heart or shut your hand against your poor brother."

The harvest you reap on your credit card purchases and bank loans is immediate, but sometimes the harvest on your seed sown could take a while! Usually, when you satisfy the immediate, you forfeit the future! Have you ever heard of the "curse of the monthly payment?" That is when we no longer count the actual total cost of something, but rather, we have learned to divide that cost into 60 equal payments and only count one of those payments as the cost! We get it in our minds that the cost is so small. After all, it is just a monthly payment. But that monthly payment keeps coming, month after month. Listen to what the Bible says in Luke 14:28. *"For which of you, desiring to build a tower, does not first sit down and count the cost, whether he has enough to complete it?"* We no longer consider whether we HAVE enough to FINISH it, but only whether we HAVE enough to START it. We have it backward.

We could go a long way to helping ourselves! You could stop buying stuff you do not need. Do not get ahead of God and try to get what you want before you have the money. That is called debt. If you let it, it will hurt you, steal your future, crush your family, and ultimately kill you with stress. You must see debt for what it is, a killing machine. This world's system is designed to drag you into debt at every possible turn. Everything you read, see, and hear is all trying to convince you that what you currently have is not good enough anymore, even if you just got it. Your phone, TV, car, business, and spouse are not good enough! After all, there is always a newer model available! There is always better out there, they say. You should not be content with what you have. After all, God would want you to have better because you are a child of Almighty God! Watch it! It is a lie. God certainly wants you to have nice things, but He wants to be the one who gets them to you, not have you finance them before it is the right time. Wait on God to bless you. Do not bless yourself and then label it as God's provision, and then complain about being in debt.

1 Timothy 6:6-9 "But godliness with contentment is great gain, for we brought nothing into the world, and we cannot take anything out of the world. But if we have food and clothing, we will be content with these. But those who desire to be rich fall into temptation, into a snare, into many senseless and harmful desires that plunge people into ruin and destruction."

Discontentment means you are unwilling to wait on God to get what you need. Contentment means; Thank You God, for what we do have, and we are willing to wait on Your timing for us to have the next thing.

Mixing faith with your giving is to believe that what God said about your situation is true, regardless of what you currently see.

There are three basic parts to a financial problem.

1. What the enemy says and does – The attack.

2. What God says and does – The authority.

3. What we say and do - The agreement.

<u>So, what does the enemy say?</u>

WARNING: This may make you mad! But you need to hear this because this is how the enemy talks to you. He does not play fair!

The enemy says things like this:

What are you going to do now? You cannot make it from here. After you lose this job, how will you feed your family then? Your parents did not do well financially, and neither will you. You have already passed your peak; you never could make it happen. You will struggle all your life with money. Your expenses will always exceed your income. Just go ahead and prepare for lack. The more you follow God, the worse it gets. You cannot have nice things; you are destined to live scraping the bottom of the barrel. Others will succeed, but you will not. Your time is now past; you have already missed the opportunities for your success. You will never get out of debt. You will never have a nice car. Expenses will continue to rise, your income will continue to decrease, and it will not improve. Better clothes for your kids - forget about it. Your business is going to flop, so why even try? By now, do you see that you do not have what it takes to start a business? Even if you got some money, you would lose it quickly. From now on, it will just be one problem after another, one breakdown after another, one failure after another. Do you get it? You are too old, inexperienced, under-educated, financially burdened, risky for promotion, and medically challenged, and nobody wants you. It is time you face reality; you will not make it. God does not want you to prosper if it is not working by now. You and your spouse are destined to struggle, and so are your children after you.

You see, the devil tries to make your future appear doubtful and to seem unpredictable, unsettled, unstable, unsteady, and uncertain.

So, what does God say? There is a practical, Godly side!

John 10:10 "The thief comes only to steal, and kill, and destroy;»

John 8:44 "He was a murderer from the beginning and does not stand in the truth, because there is no truth in him. Whenever he speaks a lie, he speaks from his own nature (native language); for he is a liar and the father of lies."

Ephesians 4:27 "…and give no opportunity to the devil."

Ephesians 6:11 "Put on the whole armor of God, that you may be able to stand against the schemes of the devil."

1 Peter 5:8 "Be sober minded; be watchful. Your adversary the devil prowls around like a roaring lion, seeking someone to devour."

James 4:7 "Submit yourselves therefore to God. Resist the devil, and he will flee from you."

Proverbs 21:5 (GNT) "Plan carefully and you will have plenty; if you act too quickly, you will never have enough."

Proverbs 21:20 (GNT) ". . . unwise people spend their money as fast as they get it."

Psalm 115:14 (KJV) "The Lord shall increase you more and more, you and your children."

Psalm 4:5 (KJV) "Offer the sacrifices of righteousness and put your trust in the Lord.

Proverbs 22:9 (AMP) "He who is generous will be blessed . . ."

Acts 20:35 "It is more blessed to give than to receive."

Philippians 4:19 "And my God will supply every need of yours according to his riches in glory in Christ Jesus."

So, the Word is clear about where God stands on the issue of your financial blessing. But that is not the only factor involved. You also have something to say about it!

So, what do you say? What is your confession?

You could go to the Word of God and say things like this . . .

"I am filled with the knowledge of God's will in all wisdom and spiritual understanding. His will is my prosperity. (Colossians 1:19; Psalm 35:27)

God delights in my prosperity. He gives me power to get wealth, that He may establish His covenant upon the earth. (Deuteronomy 8:18; 11:12)

I immediately respond in faith to the guidance of the Holy Spirit. I am always in the right place at the right time because the Lord orders my steps. (Psalm 37:23)

God has given me everything that pertains to life and godliness, and I can possess all that God has provided for me (Numbers 13:30; 2 Peter 1:3-4)

God is the unfailing, unlimited source of my supply. My financial income now increases as the blessings of the Lord overtake me. (Deuteronomy 28:2)"

As I give, it is given unto me, good measure, pressed down, shaken together, and running over. (Luke 6:38)

I honor the Lord with my substance and the first fruits of my increase. My barns are filled with plenty, and my presses burst forth with new wine. (Proverbs 3:9-10)

I am like a tree planted by rivers of water. I bring forth fruit in my season, my leaf shall not wither, and whatever I do will prosper. The grace of God even makes my mistakes prosper. (Psalm 1:3)

The blessing of the Lord truly makes me rich, and He adds no sorrow to it. (Proverbs 10:22)

My God makes all grace abound toward me in every favor and earthly blessing so that I have all sufficiency for all things and abound to every good work. (2 Corinthians 9:8)

The Lord has opened unto me His good treasure and blessed the work of my hands. He has commanded the blessing upon me in my storehouse and all I undertake. (Deuteronomy 28:8,12)

I delight myself in the Lord, and He gives me the desires of my heart. (Psalm 37:4)

The Lord has pleasure in the prosperity of His servant, and Abraham's blessings are mine. (Psalm 35:27; Galatians 3:14)

Christ has redeemed me from the curse of the law. Jesus has delivered me from poverty and given me wealth. God makes all grace (every favor and earthly blessing) come to me in abundance so that I may always and under all circumstances and whatever the need, be self-sufficient possessing enough to require no aid or support and furnished in abundance for every good work and charitable donation! Therefore, I will be enriched in all things and in every way, so that I can be generous, and my generosity, as it is administered, will bring forth thanksgiving to God. I have given, and it is given to me good measure, pressed down, shaken together, running over. Men give to me—all the time. I do not lack any good thing, for my God supplies all my needs according to His riches in glory by Christ Jesus. The Lord rebukes the devourer for my sake, and no weapon that is formed against my finances will prosper. All obstacles and hindrances to my financial prosperity are now dissolved. (Malachi 3:10, 11; Isaiah 54:17, Luke 6:38)

So, whether we are talking about your personal finances, debts, assets, start-up businesses, disappointments of the past, past failures, business failures, personal bad financial decisions, or whatever, you need to break the assignment of the enemy and speak the Word of God over your situation!

What I mean by that is that you need to pray and speak to your situation! This is where the rubber meets the road. You can talk about prayer, text others about prayer, post on social media about how much you pray, tell others that you are praying for them, have a prayer journal, get in a posture of prayer, have a prayer cloth and a prayer closet, and even memorize scriptures on prayer. But, at some point, you actually need to PRAY!

HERE IS AN EXAMPLE OF A SCRIPTURAL PRAYER:

Father, You are great, and You perform great deeds. You alone are God. We thank You for Your unfailing love for us that never ends and Your mercies which never do cease. Thank You, Father, for being our strength, shield, provider, and Savior. Thank You for blessing us with jobs that provide us with income. Thank You for the promotions and raises. Thank You for your favor with our bosses and co-workers.

Father, we confess that we will save, spend, and invest money in obedience to Your perfect plan for our lives and families. We confess that as You bring financial blessings into our lives, we will remember that You give us the power to get wealth. We declare that we are set high above the nations of the earth because we diligently obey Your voice and observe Your commandments. We say that all we put our hands to do is blessed because You have commanded blessings on our storehouses, including our savings, investments, and retirement accounts. We declare that as Your blessings overtake us, we can lend money to many without borrowing from any. As we bring the tithes into Your house, we expect You to pour out immense blessings that we will not have room to receive. Lord, we declare that we will be faithful stewards of Your financial blessings, and we expect You to confirm Your Word and make us rulers over abundant wealth. We call forth a new anointing of entrepreneurship, new ideas, and new businesses. We call forth a spirit of excellence and prosperity in our finances and all areas of our lives.

Father, we pray for promotions and financial increases. Help us to build business and personal relationships with others and give us favor with the business community. Finally, we pray for a breaking of old mindsets and generational curses of poverty and lack within our families.

Forgive us for repeating patterns of financial failures, living beyond our means, and misusing the finances you entrusted to us. Thank You for not withholding any good thing from us as we walk uprightly before You. Forgive us for words and thoughts of doubt and unbelief. Father, forgive us for walking by sight rather than walking by faith.

I challenge you to think about and say aloud the following things:

- Every mountain of lack, be removed from my path.

- Every devourer assigned to my finances be destroyed.

- Every dollar of stolen wealth, be restored to me seven-fold.

- Whatever I may have lost to the enemy, I take back by force in Jesus' name.

- You spirit of poverty, I put a stop to your activities in my life.

- God's overwhelming abundance consumes every lack in my life.

- Every power manipulating my blessings, be disarmed.

- Every seed I have sown, bring forth your assigned harvest.

- Every storm that threatens my harvest be calm.

- According to the word of God, let harvest time follow my seed time.

- Let the wealth of the ungodly be transferred unto me.

- Let my desert be turned into pools of water, and let my parched ground be turned into springs.

Now, Father, in the name of Jesus, we agree that the recession, the depression, inflation, and every other economic downfall does not belong to us! We are the children of God, not the children of the world. We are the children of light, not the children of darkness. We walk in the light as you are in the light, Lord. You are our source. Today, We grab every promise and word You said and the oath You declared to Abraham. You will perform that oath and that promise to me and my household. We declare it. We claim it. We receive it. It is done. Hallelujah. We are blessed. Glory to God. In Jesus' Name, Amen!

Questions to Consider:

1. Do either of you bring significant debt into the marriage?

_____

_____

2. Individually, are you a saver or a spender?

_____

_____

3. Will you have separate or joint checking accounts or a combination of both?

_____

_____

4. If you have separate accounts, who will be responsible for which expenses?

_____

_____

5. Who will pay the bills and ensure they are paid on time?

_____

_____

6. Do you always agree to disclose each other's financial situations fully?

_____

_____

7. Do you view going to the movies and taking an annual vacation as a necessity or a luxury?

_____

_____

8. What are your financial goals as a couple?

_____

_____

9. Do you both know the location of important financial documents?

_____

_____

10. How will you resolve disagreements about spending money?

_____

_____

11. How much money do each of you need to feel comfortable?

_____

_____

12. Will you have a savings plan for purchasing a house or a car?

_____

_____

13. What is an acceptable amount of credit card debt for each of you?

_____

_____

14. What is your plan for taking financial responsibility for the needs of your parents?

_____

_____

15. Do you plan to send your children to public or private schools?

_____

_____

16. What are your plans for funding your children's college education?

_____

_____

17. When do you plan to begin saving for retirement?

_____

_____

18. Will you work with a financial planner?

_____

_____

19. How will you manage taxes as a couple?

_____

_____

Summary:

Effectively managing money in marriage is crucial for building a healthy and thriving relationship. Properly overseeing money in marriage requires communication, teamwork, and discipline. In addition, managing money in marriage requires faith in God's provision and wisdom. Couples should trust that God will provide for their needs and guide them in their financial decisions.

Notes:

_____

_____

_____

_____

_____

_____

_____

_____

7

Relationships

Introduction:

Getting married is a significant life event that comes with many changes, including changes in relationships with parents, in-laws, and friends. While it is a joyous occasion, it can also be stressful and overwhelming, especially when navigating these relationships.

Instruction:

Did you know that you and your marriage have an assignment from heaven, and you can choose to walk in or out of it? Make sure you have godly friendships that are in their proper place. No friendship outside of your marriage should ever supersede or even overly influence the friendship and relationship between you and your spouse! You must be cautious not to fall into the trap of becoming such great friends with someone else that you begin to discuss things that only belong to you and your spouse. This is dangerous ground! Yes, have friends, but be willing to define the lines of that friendship clearly.

It is suggested that when you marry your partner, you also marry their extended family. Establishing boundaries with others after marriage is crucial for maintaining a healthy and happy relationship with your spouse. While others may mean well, they can unintentionally overstep boundaries, causing unnecessary tension and stress in your marriage. Establishing proper boundaries with others after marriage will help avoid conflicts and misunderstandings. It is essential to communicate your expectations and limits so that they understand what is and is not acceptable. When clear boundaries are in place, other people are less likely to cross them unintentionally, leading to fewer conflicts and misunderstandings.

HAVING GOOD BOUNDARIES PROMOTES PROPER INDEPENDENCE.

Marriage is a significant step and marks the start of a new chapter in life. Establishing boundaries with family members and friends after getting married can help promote independence as a couple. It allows you and your partner to make decisions together without the influence or interference of family members. This is especially important regarding finances, career choices, and children.

HAVING GOOD BOUNDARIES PROTECTS YOUR RELATIONSHIP.

Establishing boundaries is crucial for protecting your relationship. When family members overstep boundaries, it can cause tension and stress between you and your spouse, leading to resentment and conflict. Setting clear boundaries protects your marriage from unwanted interference and ensures your relationship remains strong and healthy.

HAVING GOOD BOUNDARIES ENCOURAGES MUTUAL RESPECT.

Establishing boundaries with family members after getting married encourages mutual respect. It shows that you value your relationship with your spouse and expect others to do the same. By setting boundaries, you are also demonstrating that you respect the opinions and wishes of your spouse, which is crucial for a successful marriage.

HAVING GOOD BOUNDARIES FOSTERS OPEN COMMUNICATION.

Establishing boundaries with family members after getting married fosters open communication. It encourages family members to openly and honestly communicate their needs and expectations, which can help prevent misunderstandings and conflicts. It also helps to create a supportive and respectful environment where everyone's needs are considered.

It may be challenging to set boundaries with people you also love, but it is essential to prioritize your marriage and make it clear that you and your spouse are a team. With clear and respectful communication, you can establish boundaries that work for everyone and ensure your marriage remains strong and healthy.

What about Parents?

Inevitably, at some point, you will have to face the question of setting boundaries with your parents too. Parents are a significant part of our lives, and their involvement may not necessarily decrease after we get married. Here are some tips on how to work with parents after you get married:

- **Set Boundaries:** While your parents may want to be involved in your life, it is essential to establish some boundaries. Discuss your expectations and boundaries with your parents, and be clear about what is acceptable and what is not. This will help to prevent conflicts and misunderstandings in the future.

- **Respect Their Opinions:** Your parents may have different views on family, religion, and parenting. Even if you disagree with their opinions, it is essential to respect them. Listen to their point of view and try to understand where they are coming from. This will help to maintain a positive relationship with them.

- **Communicate:** Communication is critical to maintaining a healthy relationship with your parents. Keep them informed about your life, but also be willing to listen to what they have to say. Regular communication can help to build a strong relationship with your parents.

- **Spend Time Together:** Spending time with your parents can help to strengthen your relationship. Try to visit them regularly, have dinner, or go on a trip together. This will help to create lasting memories and deepen your bond.

What about In-Laws?

Dealing with in-laws can also be challenging, especially if you have different personalities and values. Here are some tips on how to deal with in-laws after you get married:

- **Respect Them:** It is essential to show respect to your in-laws, even if you disagree with them. Be polite, courteous, and loving to avoid negative or critical remarks.

- **Set Boundaries:** Like with your parents, it is important to set boundaries with your in-laws. Discuss your expectations and be clear about what is acceptable and what is not. This will help to prevent conflicts and misunderstandings in the future.

- **Communicate:** Communication is key to healthy relationships with your in-laws. Keep them informed about your life, but also be willing to listen to what they have to say. Regular communication can help to build a strong relationship with your in-laws.

- **Find Common Ground:** Try to find common ground with your in-laws. For example, find shared interests or hobbies that you can do together. This will help to create a positive and enjoyable relationship with your in-laws.

What about Friends?

Getting married can also affect your friendships. Here are some tips on how to deal with friends after you get married:

- **Prioritize Your Marriage:** While it is important to maintain your friendships, your marriage should be your top priority. Therefore, spend time with your partner and prioritize your relationship.

- **Stay in Touch:** Stay connected with your friends, even just a quick text or phone call. This will help to maintain your friendships and prevent them from fading away.

- **Be Inclusive:** Include your friends in your life and events, such as dinners or parties. This will help to maintain your friendships and show that you still value them.

- **Be Understanding:** Understand that your friends may have different priorities and lifestyles than you do. Be understanding if they cannot hang out as much or have different interests. This will help to maintain a positive relationship with your friends.

Mark 10:6-9 "But from the beginning of creation, God made them male and female. Therefore, a man shall leave his father and mother and hold fast to his wife, and the two shall become one flesh. So, they are no longer two but one flesh. What therefore God has joined together, let not man separate."

In other words, let no man untwist, untangle, unbraid, unravel, unwind, or unthread you. But, you know, it is up to you to make sure no other person or situation is allowed to separate you. That is your job.

Questions to Consider:

1. How do you feel about your partner's family?

_____

_____

2. How much time do you and your partner plan to spend with your respective parents?

_____

_____

3. What are your holiday plans, and where do you plan to spend them?

_____

_____

4. Can you predict the holiday expectations of each of your parents, and how do you plan to address those expectations?

_____

_____

5. What type of support do you expect from your partner when your parents pressure you to do something?

_____

_____

6. Is it acceptable for either of you to discuss any relationship issues with your parents?

_____

_____

7. What type of relationship do you expect your children to have with your parents?

_____

_____

8. Do you foresee a situation in which you will want a parent to live with the two of you as they age or require assistance?

_____

_____

Summary:

While marriage is supposed to be a joyous occasion, it can also be stressful and overwhelming, especially when navigating the various relationships that still attempt to influence you and your time. Therefore, setting specific boundaries to protect your time and marriage is important. It may initially seem challenging to set boundaries with people you also love, but it is essential to prioritize your marriage and make it clear that you and your spouse are a team. With clear and respectful communication, you can establish boundaries that work for everyone and ensure your marriage remains strong and healthy.

Notes:

_____

_____

_____

_____

_____

_____

_____

_____

_____

_____

_____

_____

8

Children

Introduction:

Having children after marriage is a BIG decision that many couples face. The Bible speaks of children as a blessing from the Lord and encourages couples to raise them in a godly way. Let us explore the biblical perspective on having children after marriage.

Instruction:

First, the Bible clearly states that children are a blessing from God. Psalm 127:3-5 says, *"Behold, children are a heritage from the Lord, the fruit of the womb a reward. Like arrows in the hand of a warrior are the children of one's youth. Blessed is the man who fills his quiver with them! He shall not be put to shame when he speaks with his enemies in the gate."* This scripture describes children as a reward to be treasured and valued. It also speaks of the importance of raising them well, as arrows in the hands of a warrior. Children are not a burden but rather a blessing from God.

Second, the Bible teaches that marriage is the foundation for starting a family. Genesis 1:27-28 says, *"So God created man in his own image, in the image of God he created him; male and female he created them. And God blessed them. And God said to them, 'Be fruitful and multiply and fill the earth and subdue it.'"* This passage shows that the ability to bear children is a gift from God and that he has given it to married couples to fulfill his command to be fruitful and multiply. Children are an essential part of God's plan for the world, and starting a family within the context of marriage is the best way to honor that plan.

Third, the Bible teaches that children are to be raised in a godly way. Deuteronomy 6:6-7 says, *"And these words that I command you today shall be on your heart. You shall teach them diligently to your children and shall talk of them when you sit in your house, and when you walk by the way, and when you lie down, and when you rise."* This scripture shows that parents are responsible for instructing their children about God and his ways. This means children should be raised in an environment that promotes godly values and principles. Parents should strive to create a home where their children can grow up in a secure and loving environment that nurtures their spiritual growth.

Fourth, the Bible teaches that children are a gift from God and should be treated as such. For example, Psalm 127:3 says, *"Behold, children are a heritage from the Lord, the fruit of the womb a reward."* This Bible verse shows children should be valued and cherished as God-given gifts. Therefore, parents should treat their children with love and respect and should strive to raise them in a way that honors God.

The Bible teaches that having children after marriage is a blessing from God. Children are a gift from God and should be treated as such. The Bible also teaches that marriage is the foundation for starting a family and that children should be raised in a godly way. As Christians, we should honor God by raising our children in a way that reflects his love and values. We should never forget that children are a precious gift from God, and we should do our best to raise them to be godly men and women.

Questions to Consider:

1. What are your thoughts on having children? Are they similar or different from your partner's?

_____

_____

2. If you have differences on this subject, what plans do you have to reconcile them?

_____

_____

3. Have you discussed how long you want to be married before having children?

_____

_____

4. What are your thoughts on the kind of parents you will be?

_____

_____

6. Have you talked about your parenting philosophy?

_____

_____

7. Do you have a preference for the age gap between your children?

_____

_____

8. What is your stance on pro-life and abortion? Would you ever consider abortion as an option?

_____

_____

9. Have you discussed the philosophies you want to incorporate into child raising? Do you both agree?

_____

_____

10. How do you plan to shape your children's values and beliefs?

_____

_____

11. What types of punishment or discipline do you believe are appropriate or inappropriate?

_____

_____

12. What expectations do you have about the money spent on toys, clothes, and other items for your children?

_____

_____

13. How do you plan to prevent spoiling your children and maintain a healthy balance in their upbringing?

_____

_____

Summary:

No matter your thoughts on children, you need to understand that God says children are a blessing directly from Him. God also says that children are a gift from Him. Therefore, as Christians, we should honor God by raising our children in a way that reflects his love and values.

Notes:

_____

_____

_____

_____

_____

_____

_____

_____

_____

_____

_____

_____

_____

_____

9

A Thriving Christian Marriage

A thriving Christian marriage is one where both partners prioritize their relationship with God and seek to honor Him in every aspect of their relationship. This means being available for prayer, studying the Bible together, attending church regularly, and serving others in their community.

In this kind of marriage, couples support each other's spiritual growth, encouraging and challenging each other to pursue a deeper relationship with God. They recognize that their marriage is about their happiness and reflecting God's love and grace to others.

Communication is vital, as couples openly share their thoughts and feelings while listening actively and empathetically. You should seek to understand each other's perspectives and respond with love and respect, even in moments of disagreement or conflict.

Forgiveness and grace are also essential in a thriving marriage, as you recognize that you both have flaws and are recipients of God's grace.

Therefore, make every attempt to extend the same grace and forgiveness to each other that God has shown you, seeking reconciliation and restoration when conflicts arise.

A thriving spiritual marriage is built on a foundation of love and commitment to God and each other. This partnership honors God and seeks to bring Him glory through every aspect of their lives together.

Instruction:

SEVEN THINGS THAT ARE ESSENTIAL FOR A THRIVING MARRIAGE!

1. **You need God**. You must first acknowledge your need for God to make your marriage work. You cannot rely solely on your strength, resources, or wisdom. Instead, you must trust God with your whole heart, soul, and mind and seek His guidance, presence, and power in your marriage. You need to pray together, read the Bible, worship, and follow God's plan together. When you build your marriage on a foundation of faith, hope, and love in God, you can withstand any storm and enjoy any blessing that comes your way.

2. **You need God's Word**. You must also feed your marriage with God's Word to keep it strong and healthy. The Bible is not just a book of rules but a treasure of wisdom, inspiration, and revelation that can transform your thinking, feeling, and acting. You need to study the Word together, meditate on it day and night, memorize it, apply it, and share it. The Word will help you discern God's will, your heart, your spouse's needs, and the lies and temptations of the world, the flesh, and the devil. When you renew your mind with the truth of God, you can experience the fullness of life and love that God has prepared for you.

3. **You need your spouse**. It seems like this would be an easy decision - you need your spouse in your marriage! You should have a mutual need for each other. You cannot live as independent individuals who happen to share a house or a bed. You must live as interdependent partners who complement, support and cherish

each other. You need to listen to each other, communicate honestly and respectfully, forgive, serve, and celebrate each other. You must understand each other's strengths and weaknesses, dreams and fears, preferences and priorities, and learn how to blend them into a beautiful harmony. When you cherish your spouse as a gift from God and invest your time, energy, and resources in your marriage, you can create a lifelong bond of love that honors God and blesses others. 1 Corinthians 11:11 *"Nevertheless, in the Lord woman is not independent of man nor man of woman,"* Ephesian 5:25 (Message) - *"Husbands, go all out in your love for your wives, exactly as Christ did for the church — a love marked by giving, not getting."* Husbands, you need to recognize how much you need your wife! Wives, you need to recognize how much you need your husband!

4. **You need the church body**. The Body of Christ is essential to your spiritual life. Romans 12:3-5 says, *"We are all part of one body, with different functions and abilities, but united in Christ."* When you isolate yourself from the church community, you deprive yourself and others of the support, encouragement, and growth that come from being a part of the Body. You need others, and others need you.

5. **You need to be in church**. Attending church regularly is necessary for spiritual growth. As Hebrews 10:23-25 reminds us, *"We should not neglect gathering together as believers, but instead, we should encourage and spur each other on to love and good works."* Observing the Sabbath day and setting aside time for worship is a way of honoring God and strengthening your faith. **Men, leading your family to church is an integral part of demonstrating godly leadership and setting an example for your family.** Wives supporting your husband and family in regular church attendance shows that you prioritize God in your family life and strengthen the unity of your family. It is an enormously powerful thing!

6. **You need to be involved.** Jesus came to serve, and we become more like Him every time we serve others, including our spouse. We were created for service, and God has blessed us with different gifts and abilities to serve one another. In 1 Peter 4:10, we are instructed to

serve one another with the gifts we have received. When you shift from an "I could not care less" attitude to active involvement in church, momentum shifts. You begin to take ownership, and your level of care skyrockets. Suddenly, you notice the gum wrapper on the carpet and feel compelled to pick it up, see the lady struggling to carry her baby seat, the man on crutches trying to climb the stairs, and the frustration and tears on the faces of parents who had a rough morning, and you begin to weep too! Why? Because you are involved, you care, and the love of God is being shed abroad in your heart by the Holy Ghost. You need to be fully engaged in your marriage, in service to each other, and service to others. I have a firefighter friend named Rick. I always enjoy learning something from a professional who is exceptionally good at their job. So, one day I asked Rick what he could share with me that was meaningful. He went on to tell me about the four levels of a house fire! See if you can relate to this since we are discussing involvement.

The four levels are as follows:

1. Nothing is showing — just a little smoldering, but no real, visible signs of any activity happening.

2. Light smoke — the very beginning signs of some activity are visible.

3. Some flame — definite signs of limited activity, but only occasionally.

4. Fully involved — completely visible, easy to see, no doubt. "Fully Involved" typically refers to being actively and wholeheartedly engaged. This refers to being fully committed and invested in one's marriage, giving it full attention, effort, and energy.

Well, I am glad I talked to Rick that day. I do not know if I have ever heard a more concise explanation. You need to be fully involved in your marriage!

7. **You need to keep moving.** Hebrews 12:1-3 encourages us to lay aside every encumbrance and sin that entangles us and run with endurance the race set before us. We should fix our eyes on Jesus,

the author, and perfecter of our faith, who endured the cross and sat down at the right hand of God. We will not grow weary and lose heart when considering what He endured. Stay on course, lock arms with your spouse, commit, and stay faithful to God and His Word, and you will finish this race.

Questions to Consider:

1. Do you both share the same basic spiritual values?

_____

_____

2. Do you expect him or her to change and move toward your values after marriage?

_____

_____

3. Is it easy or difficult for you to pray with your partner? Why?

_____

_____

4. What are the primary issues you continue to disagree and argue over?

_____

_____

5. How are you working out these differences?

_____

_____

6. What does spirituality mean to each of you?

_____

_____

7. What about your church attendance? Is this essential to you both?

_____

_____

8. Will you attend regular Bible studies to grow spiritually?

_____

_____

9. Will you read the Bible regularly?

_____

_____

10. How will you share with each other things that are important to you?

_____

_____

11. Will your children be expected to attend church services?

_____

_____

12. Will you send your children to a Christian school?

_____

_____

13. Will the children go through baptism?

_____

_____

14. Is it important to you to have a church home that you attend?

_____

_____

15. Is there a certain person you consider your pastor?

_____

_____

Summary:

A thriving Christian marriage has many benefits for both partners. Keeping God first place in your marriage will strengthen you emotionally, spiritually, and physically. As a result, you can experience increased happiness and satisfaction in life. A good Christian marriage also provides solid support for children and can serve as a witness of God's love for others. This partnership honors God and brings joy, meaning, and purpose to both partners' lives.

Notes:

_____

_____

_____

_____

_____

_____

_____

_____

_____

_____

10

Extramarital Relationships

Entering an extramarital relationship seriously violates the commitment that God intends for marriage. The Bible teaches that marriage is a covenant between one man and one woman and that infidelity is a sin against God and one's spouse.

Instruction:

The book of Proverbs warns against the dangers of adultery, stating, Proverbs 5:3-4 (NIV), *"For the lips of an adulteress drip honey, and her speech is smoother than oil; but in the end she is bitter as gall, sharp as a double-edged sword."* This passage highlights the deceitful nature of an extramarital relationship, which may seem sweet and enticing at first, but ultimately leads to pain and destruction.

The apostle Paul also warns against sexual immorality, stating in 1 Corinthians 6:18 (NIV), *"Flee from sexual immorality. All other sins a person commits are outside the body, but whoever sins sexually sins against their own body.* "This passage emphasizes the seriousness of engaging in sexual activity outside of marriage, which can have physical and spiritual consequences.

And the Bible also teaches the importance of faithfulness and commitment in marriage. For example, in the book of Malachi, God speaks against the unfaithfulness of the Israelites, stating, in Malachi 2:16 (NIV), *"The man who hates and divorces his wife... does violence to the one he should protect."* This passage highlights the importance of protecting and honoring one's spouse rather than engaging in behavior that harms the marriage covenant.

From the beginning of your marriage, it is up to you to establish that affairs are not an option for you! As believers in Christ, we are to avoid sin at all costs! This is necessary, and it is up to you to see that one another avoids falling into the trap of sin! Do not seek sin! Do not even prepare for sin.

By the time you get into sin, you have already taken several steps to reach that point. You do not just start out seeking sin, hoping to ruin your life and your family. It takes several steps in the wrong direction to get to the point where an extramarital, adulterous affair happens. It comes one step at a time, and you have a choice all along the way with how you handle things. Here are those steps of progression that lead to sin:

1. It all starts with a "**Leak.**" This is when you choose not to stay full of God, to remain spiritually in tune, full of the Word of God and Prayer. This has a profound negative effect on your life. You may have even had it all together at one point, but then, due to laziness, you lose it. You chose to sin and wrongdoing right here!

2. Next, you become "**Weak.**" This is when spiritual weakness sets in. This is when you become liable to break or give way under pressure easily. You cannot handle it. You were supposed to remain strong and courageous, but you became weak because of the leak in step number one.

3. Of course, the next step is the "**Sneak.**" When you must start moving about stealthily, you find yourself looking both ways before you

look at something wrong. Eventually, you start hiding your actions so that no one around you will see what you are up to or the direction you are taking. You know you are in trouble when you need to conceal your actions!

4. With all this sneaking around, the next obvious step is to take a **"Peek."** Just a glance is all it takes to get the ball rolling. Juices start flowing when you take the time to glance at something or someone just long enough to be compelling. Unfortunately, this is leading to real trouble.

5. The last step in this downward spiral is the **"Seek."** Now you are in real trouble. You have run all the roadblocks and stop signs and started seeking sin. You have reached the place where your desires have overcome you, thrown your character away, and now you are just going for it. Ouch! All of this could have been avoided by taking care of step number one.

You see, trouble can come at you from any angle, anytime, through people, situations, the devil, and even yourself. Problems do come, and you cannot stop them from coming, but you can respond properly. But if you are ever going to deal with the trouble or troubling times properly, you must first realize that you and your marriage are not exempt from risk. You do not have a free pass on hardship. Job 14:1 *"Man who is born of a woman is few of days and full of trouble."* Troubles come, but they do not have to stay.

Psalms 46:1 God is our refuge and strength, a very present help in trouble.

Trouble and temptation also go hand in hand. Temptation means trouble is ahead! One day at my house, I was opening my mail, and opened this one piece, only to find it was full of pornographic advertising. Porn mail came directly to my house. My wife was right there with me, so I immediately closed the envelope and handed it to her. Then we went inside the house and shredded it. But there I was, minding my own business, opening mail from my mailbox, and paying bills, and trouble came right to me.

Without me asking for it and without me knowing it was coming. Trouble can come to you at any time. Your job is to be prepared!

There are several types of troubles to consider too. One is trouble caused by disobedience, which occurs when someone violates the law or goes against God's known Word. Another is trouble due to ignorance, caused by an honest mistake due to a lack of knowledge. Additionally, trouble can come unexpectedly, such as receiving inappropriate mail. And there is the trouble one brings by failing to adhere to a budget and consequently incurring debt. Troubling times, such as societal issues, riots, storms, and floods, also fall into this category. Lastly, some individuals intentionally cause trouble, known as troublemakers.

HERE ARE SOME WAYS THAT TROUBLE CAN TAKE HOLD IN YOUR MARRIAGE:

1. Unrealistic expectations - When one or both partners hold unrealistic expectations, it can create unnecessary pressure, disappointment, and conflict within the marriage. It is essential to remember that everyone is human and has flaws. Colossians 3:23-24 reminds us to do everything we do for the Lord and not for people, acknowledging that our true reward comes from Him, not our spouses.

2. Unachievable goals - Setting unrealistic goals beyond the couple's abilities and resources can cause frustration and disappointment. Setting achievable goals that align with the couple's values, priorities, and resources is vital. Proverbs 16:3 encourages us to commit our plans to the Lord, and they will succeed.

3. Unannounced desires - When one spouse has unannounced desires, it can create confusion and conflict in the marriage. Communicating openly and honestly with your spouse about your desires and expectations is essential. Proverbs 15:1 reminds us that a soft answer turns wrath away, but a harsh word stirs anger.

4. Unfulfilled passion - When passion is left unfulfilled in the marriage, it can lead to loneliness and dissatisfaction. Prioritizing intimacy and regularly communicating about each other's needs and desires

is essential. 1 Corinthians 7:3-5 emphasizes that the husband and wife should fulfill each other's physical needs within the marriage.

5. Unresolved conflict - When conflicts arise in the marriage and are left unresolved, they can fester and cause bitterness and resentment. It is important to address conflicts and work together toward a resolution. Proverbs 18:13 emphasizes that listening to both sides before forming an opinion is vital for resolving disputes.

6. Unexpected setbacks - Unexpected setbacks, such as job loss, illness, or financial difficulties, can strain the marriage. It is crucial to support each other during challenging times and trust in God's plan. Proverbs 3:5-6 tells us to trust the Lord with all our hearts and lean not on our understanding.

7. Unspoken frustrations - When frustrations are left unspoken, it can create tension and distance within the marriage. Communicating openly and honestly with your spouse about your feelings and emotions is essential. Ephesians 4:26-27 encourages us not to let the sun go down while we are still angry, so we do not give the devil a foothold in our marriage.

Following these biblical principles can strengthen our marriage and honor our commitment to God and our spouse.

You might be in trouble if:

- You stop reading God's Word consistently or stop praying consistently.

- You think of yourself more highly than you ought.

- You prepare for and make provision for future sin.

- You put up with "just a little" arguing, yelling, or temptation.

- You take the advice of an unbeliever over a believer.

- You will not listen to or adhere to godly counsel or leadership.

- You seek much counsel from many people to get your desired answer.

- You spend time together with unbelievers more than believers.

- You listen to what unbelievers listen to, drink what they drink, watch what they watch, and sleep where they sleep.

- You openly disobey the laws of the land.

- You ask for your spouse's suggestion or advice, having already pre-determined not to take it.

- You run to your spouse's past during an argument or confrontation.

- You quickly point out your spouse's mistakes and flaws to make yourself look better.

- You absolutely must have the last word.

- When your spiritual expectations of your spouse outweigh their ability to live everyday life. Be spiritually minded! Do not be **overly** spiritually minded! If everything is about a vision or dream, about the seals being opened, the Glory of the Lord ascending and descending, but you do not have time to make dinner, repair the house, or have sex, you are in trouble!

So, you need to know that the Lord intends to deliver you from all your troubles! Second Chronicles 15:4 "*But when in their distress they turned to the LORD, the God of Israel, and sought him, he was found by them.*" Then, right away, you must decide that you will not let your heart be troubled. *You* don't let your heart be troubled. God gave you a choice. God gave YOU power over your heart. Many people believe that in each situation, there is no way they can help but remain in trouble, to be depressed, and to be discouraged. But this is contrary to God's Word. To "let not" is a command as much as any other command in the Word — as much as "thou shalt not commit adultery, thou shalt not steal, and thou shalt not kill." It is a direct command from the Lord! So, you have to say, "I am not going to let my heart be troubled."

It does not matter what comes your way — physical problems, financial problems, relationship problems — whatever the devil is fighting you with. God has given you the ability to overcome it. But you must choose that. If you identify with troubles, discouragement, doubt, and depression, you set a precedent that will enslave you for the rest of your life.

Questions to Consider:

1. Do you agree that an emotional affair is equal to a sexual affair?

    _____

    _____

2. Do you have thoughts of what it would be like to be married to someone else?

    _____

    _____

3. In your relationship, has there ever been any unfaithfulness?

    _____

    _____

4. Have either of you been actively involved in viewing pornography?

    _____

    _____

5. What is the status of your pornography use?

    _____

    _____

6. Will you commit to never talking to a person of the opposite sex (except a therapist or clergy) about your relationship with your partner since this builds a bond outside of your relationship?

    _____

    _____

Summary:

Engaging in an extramarital relationship seriously violates God's design for marriage. The Bible warns against the dangers of adultery, emphasizes the importance of faithfulness and commitment, and reminds us that sexual immorality is a sin against God and one's spouse. Therefore, couples must prioritize their commitment to each other, honor the sanctity of marriage, and seek forgiveness and restoration in times of difficulty or temptation.

Notes:

_____

_____

_____

_____

_____

_____

_____

_____

_____

_____

_____

_____

_____

11

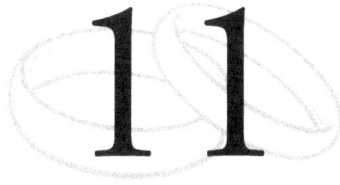

The Responsibility of Marriage

We are only given a brief period to make crucial, life-changing, eternal decisions that will affect our spouse, family, and generations to come. We talk so much about what will be accomplished in our lifetime and so little about our death-time! It is not popular or fun, but it is crucial!

You know, it does not even make sense that you could find your lovely wife, somehow talk her into marrying you, living with you, cooking for you, cleaning your underwear, having sex with you, bearing your children, and then not provide a legal means of protecting it all when you die! That is not responsible.

You can love somebody or say that you love somebody, but where is the legal paperwork to back up the extension of that love? This is about your life; this is your spouse's life, your children's life. Whether you accept it or not, you live your life right now. You do not get another one here on earth. And the last time I checked, here in America and worldwide, the death rate was holding steady at 100%. You cannot necessarily predict how your life will end or where it will end, but one thing is for sure, one of these days, it will end. It is appointed unto man to die and is coming at some point. The question is: Are you prepared for it?

Instruction:

It has been said that a person will spend fifty or sixty years accumulating earthly treasure, then spend another 20 years or more trying to keep from losing it but will spend less than two hours planning the distribution of it when he dies. Therefore, preparation for life after your death should be one of the top items on your to-do list as you prepare for marriage. You will never know how much hurt it will bring your spouse if you have not prepared. You will not have to go through anything because you will be gone, but your spouse will be here. If you genuinely love somebody, you will do what it takes to prepare for their future too responsibly.

The question has been asked many times before, "Will your widow live as well as your wife?"

If you do not already have this nailed down, you must get a will and a living trust going right now! Show your family that you love and care for them enough to provide for them if you should go. Depending on where you live, things could get sticky if you do not have a will. It could mean spending a long time in court and cost your spouse a lot of time and money.

As a married couple, it is essential to have a plan in place to ensure that your assets and financial affairs are handled smoothly in the event of one spouse's passing. A will is a legal document that outlines how your assets will be distributed upon your death, while a living trust is a legal entity that can hold and distribute assets during your lifetime and after death. Having both a will and a living trust can ensure that your assets will be handled according to your wishes and can prevent family disputes or legal challenges. In addition, by taking responsibility for your financial affairs and having a plan, you can provide peace of mind for yourself and your loved ones.

I am aware of the arguments against this too. You might say, "I cannot afford to do all that!" **You cannot afford not to.** Even if you started by writing a will on paper and getting it notarized, that would be better than not having one. You can afford all the other things in your life. You can afford cable TV, smartphones, advanced data plans, cellular hotspots, specialty coffees, aluminum alloy wheels, fashion clothes, manicures, bass boats, car washes, and pets, but not life insurance? If you have a pet, you could have life insurance! Which one would you rather have? You really cannot afford life insurance? Look your spouse in the eye tonight and tell them you love them but are unwilling to secure their financial future. You can afford it, but it might mean some sacrifice on your part to do it.

You may say, "I do not have much to leave." Well, guess what? You will leave it all, and your family might want ALL of the little you leave instead of having it eaten up in probate court. It has also been said that "The deceased will rest in peace, but the spouse may lose the house!"

Questions to Consider:

1. Do you care about your future spouse? Of course, you do! Then take care of this.

_____

_____

2. Do you want to see your spouse make it financially if you pass away? Of course, you do! Then take care of this.

_____

_____

3. Do you want to see your spouse suffer and face lack after you pass? Of course not! Then take care of this.

_____

_____

4. Do you want your future children to know that you did not do what it took to help them? Of course not! Then take care of this.

_____

_____

5. Do you want me to go on and on about your responsibility? Of course not! Then take care of this.

_____

_____

Summary:

Married couples need to have a will and living trust in place. These legal documents ensure that your assets and money are distributed how you want them to be after one of you passes away. A will is a plan that outlines who gets what, while a living trust can manage and distribute your assets while you are alive or after you are gone. By taking care of these critical matters, you can avoid any family disputes or legal issues in the future. So, ensure you secure your financial future and give yourselves peace of mind knowing everything is in order.

Notes:

_____

_____

_____

12

Committing to Stay Married

So much emphasis is placed on the wedding ceremony, the dress, the flowers, the location, the tuxedo, the lighting, etc. It is all about the start. That is okay if there is a balance in maintaining the marriage. **The wedding is a ceremony, but the marriage is a celebration!** More emphasis should be placed on maintaining and finishing. I have seen some wonderful and expensive weddings over the years, but that is just the start, just the beginning. Many of those beautiful weddings have marriages that are now no longer! Even though people spend thousands and tens of thousands of dollars on the wedding, more time is needed to maintain the marriage. The start can be great, but the finish is still more important.

Instruction:

I am always amazed at how people who have been married for a long time can easily fall into the trap of thinking they have it all together. No problems are on the horizon, and they are somehow exempt from marriage maintenance. Be careful when you stand, lest you fall. Do not take your marriage for granted. It must be maintained. You are not exempt from temptation; you are not exempt from stress, financial pressure, child pressure, job pressure, medical pressure, or time pressure at any age or any point in your marriage. Even if you have been married for quite a while, it can be easy to relax your marriage responsibilities, and before you know it, you have a problem. So, no mature or secure marriage is exempt from pressure, temptation, and attack. But at the same time, every marriage has a 100% chance of complete success if you do it God's way! I am not telling you this to scare you, make you feel insecure, or unstable, but to ensure you understand that God's principles in His Word are for everyone, not just newlyweds!

HERE ARE SOME STEP-BY-STEP INSTRUCTIONS ON "HOW TO STAY MARRIED."

Step 1: Do not get divorced!

It sounds simple enough, but obviously, it takes some doing too. Nobody likes to talk about divorce, but we must approach it head-on! If the option of divorce is on the table, you will eventually take it. Sure, it might not happen right away, but if it continues to be an option, the devil will align the circumstances so that the atmosphere is at least favorable for divorce.

Almost all couples go into marriage pledging to stay together through thick and thin. "Till death do us part," "to have and to hold from this day forward, for better, for worse, for richer, for poorer, in sickness and health, to love and to cherish, until we are parted by death. This is my solemn vow." Yet fewer and fewer couples seem willing to honor that promise.

Married couples today are under more stress and have faced more temptation than ever. Mainly because of this, people are simply afraid of committing to marriage. It starts with the fear of committing to getting married, and then it graduates to the fear of keeping the commitment to stay married.

But the most disturbing statistic on marriage comes from an updated study by the National Center for Family and Demographic Research at Bowling Green University, titled "Age Variation in the Divorce Rate, 1990 & 2017," which shows that the overall U.S. divorce rate has declined only slightly over the past three decades. And the divorce rate for those aged 50 and older has more than doubled since 1990. This profile update combines the 1990 U.S. Vital Statistics data and the 2017 American Community Survey. For those aged 45 and older, divorce rates were higher in 2017 than in 1990.

And at the same time, the overall divorce ratio in America is declining rapidly, but only because fewer and fewer are deciding to get married. It used to be called "Shacking-Up!" Now it is called cohabitation! It is the "un-covenant covenant." Couples choose to live together and share some things without a real commitment to each other. Yet, the Bible still calls it sin, no matter what you call it.

So, I am saying, "Remove the option of divorce altogether!" "Take it completely off the table." Let your spouse know that it is not an option for you, That it never will be an option, that you are not willing to go there, and that this marriage is forever! You need to tell them that! Then, from that time forward, do not entertain divorce, do not talk about divorce, do not think about divorce, do not argue about divorce, and do not use divorce as leverage to get what you want. You get the picture!

If you have divorced in the past, and you are preparing to marry now, then the person you are currently engaged to must be the only love of your life, your eternal mate! You start where you are and move forward from here! Divorce should not and cannot be an option if you are going to get married and <u>stay married</u>!

Step 2: It is time to lower your standards!

Your partner is the one you chose; they are not the one you saw in the ad, on TV, or in that movie! If you knew all the flaws that all those perfectly tanned, beautiful people had, they would never even get your attention! There are not enough surgeries, pills, or acting classes to get you or your spouse to be like all the unrealistic, false advertisements. Every picture of every man and every woman is edited to an unbelievable level. Those models often do not even end up with the original body parts but have someone else's eyes, lips, legs, or butt. Everything is stretched, toned, plumped, and manipulated in computer software. Those supermodels have been lifted, tucked, and puffed in all the right places to give you an even attainable appearance. It is not; in fact, it is not even real! And those smooth-talking male actors and models have certainly got spray-on tans too! It is all fake!

Now am I saying that it is okay just to stay ugly? To never exercise, eat right, put make-up on, or be a sweet talker? No! I am not saying you are ugly; I am saying God made you! He did not mess up when He made you, and if He had a second shot at making you again. . . He would do it again, exactly how He did it to begin with! Husbands and wives, do not expect your spouse to be someone else; they are God's design and perfect creation, and He made them just for you! Glory to God! God knew what I would need, and He made my wife specifically for me! Indeed, it would be best to take care of yourself, but not to the point that you are obsessed with trying to be like somebody else. Do what you can do to please your future spouse with your appearance, practice good hygiene, comb your hair, brush your teeth, and trim your nose hair. But when you see your future spouse, know that "that is the one for you!" That is your Mr. Dreamy; that is your supermodel!

So, when I say that it is time to lower your standards, I mean lower your worldly standard, and take on the standards of God's Word.

Step 3: Your partner is so needy!

Your partner is completely different from you. They have different emotions, desires, body parts, and unique needs. It is up to you to learn and understand the differences. When God made Adam, he made him whole but not complete! He needed Eve. Eve was not just another creation; she was the completion of a creation God had already started. Adam needed Eve, and Eve needed Adam. It is a covenant thing.

Everything about our society tells us to guard our independence, look after ourselves, seek what will meet our own needs, and not let anyone get in our way. But God tells us the exact opposite.

I heard someone put it this way:

- Society tells us marriage is about finding the right person.

- God tells us marriage is about being the right person.

- Culture tells us marriage is about meeting our own needs.

- God tells us marriage is about sacrificing your needs for your spouse.

- The world tells us marriage is about happiness.

- God tells us marriage is about holiness.

- God tells us that if you want to find yourself, you do it by losing yourself in service to others. It is in losing yourself that you find true contentment and joy. There is no better example than the marriage covenant.

In scripture, God gave us the perfect formula for a happy, divorce-free marriage. It does not take any particular skill or ability to understand. It certainly does not take a Bible scholar to interpret it. It is a simple plan that reveals the secret to a marriage filled with hope and purpose and completely indestructible. What it does take is a willing heart and a humble spirit. The problem is that this part of scripture has gotten a bad rap from husbands <u>and</u> wives due to misunderstanding. Therefore, despite desperately needing it, it is often skipped over because of its wording. Finally, this plan is laid out for us in the fifth chapter of Ephesians.

Ephesians 5:21–25, 28–29, 33 "Submitting to one another out of reverence for Christ. Wives, submit to your own husbands, as to the Lord. For the husband is the head of the wife even as Christ is the head of the church, his body, and is himself its Savior. Now as the church submits to Christ, so also wives should submit in everything to their husbands. Husbands, love your wives, as Christ loved the church and gave himself up for her; in the same way, husbands should love their wives as their own bodies. He who loves his wife loves himself. For no one ever hated his own flesh, but nourishes and cherishes it, just as Christ does the church; however, let each of you love his wife as himself, and let the wife see that she respects her husband."

Like it or not, Ephesians chapter five is in the Bible. God inspired it, man wrote it down, and we can read it. It is not going away. It never needs to go away! It is the model for marriage. So, I want to be upfront with you and tell you that I will not back down on Ephesians chapter five because some people do not care for it or do not like what it says! I hope you can appreciate that, but I will not stop referring to it even if you cannot!

In the Ephesians five model of marriage, women are told, "*Submit yourselves to your own husbands as you do to the Lord*" (v. 22). Many women today recoil at the thought of submitting, but probably only because we have misconstrued what it means to submit. But, you know, sometimes you can gauge what you believe by whose side you take when something is in question.

Women, if the thought of submitting to a man makes you sick to your stomach, you may just believe more what lesbians believe than God's Word. The LGBT crowd (lesbian, gay, bisexual & transgender) that's girls that like girls, boys that like boys, boys and girls that like boys and girls, and boys and girls that no longer consider themselves a boy or a girl but want the best of both worlds simultaneously! Is that plain enough for you?

That crowd has spent decades getting it ingrained into society that women do not ever need a man, period. That is not what God's Word says. You see it everywhere, in almost every ad now. The man cannot figure out how to turn on the TV or screw in a lightbulb, so the woman must come to help the stupid idiot out.

When we submit ourselves to Jesus, we do not fear being dominated, controlled, or abused. Instead, we are giving him a place of honor, respect, and leadership in our lives. In this same spirit of humility, women are told to submit to their husbands. To hold them in a place of honor, respect, and leadership. Not to become subservient or allow themselves to be abused but to treat their husbands with admiration and esteem.

I know this is not easy, especially with husbands who have done little to deserve their wives' respect. Many women quickly say, "If I gave my husband that honor, all it would do is encourage him to keep being bad!" Most of their time is spent nagging and complaining to discourage irresponsible behavior. One wife said, "If he ever starts acting like Jesus, I will be happy to treat him like Jesus." Women are afraid of giving respect to a man whom they feel does not deserve it because it just might make things worse.

Whenever I talk to couples about the Ephesians chapter five model, neither the husband nor the wife wants to be the first to change their behavior. A natural defense mechanism kicks in, and they immediately become hesitant and fearful.

Jimmy Evans says, "But one thing I have never seen in the passage is a disclaimer. God never tells wives to submit to their husbands only when they deserve it. He never tells husbands to be loving and sacrificial after they get the respect they need. The Christian life is not about reacting to others based on their behavior. It is about responding to others according to the principles of Scripture, regardless of how we are treated. You and I are called to a higher standard of behavior. As Christians, we commit to being imitators of Christ. To turn the other cheek when we have been wronged. To treat others as we would have them treat us. To put the needs of others above our own needs. You and I are called to live according to our faith, regardless of our circumstances and what those around us choose to do. The Ephesians 5 model of marriage is an extension of that calling. *We respond to our mate based on the principles God set before us, regardless of how our mate responds.*"

When a husband steps out in faith and begins loving and nurturing his wife the way God intended, the wife starts to soften. Before long, she treats him with the respect and dignity he always longed for. She begins submitting to his leadership and trusting him to make wise choices.

When a wife takes the initiative and starts treating her husband with respect and honor, he starts living up to her expectations. He begins leading with integrity and character. He starts to become the man she longs to have.

Questions to Consider:

1. Are you ready to completely submit yourself to your future spouse?

_____

_____

2. Are you ready to accept your future spouse just as they are?

_____

_____

3. Do you understand that your partner is imperfect, and I will still make some mistakes?

_____

_____

4. Do you also know that you are not perfect?

_____

_____

5. Do you genuinely believe that this marriage is forever?

_____

_____

6. Are you completely willing to remove the word divorce from your vocabulary?

_____

_____

7. Are you ready to commit yourself to helping your future spouse in every way you can?

_____

_____

8. Are you ready to begin learning and understanding the differences that each of you has, working toward a common goal of building a strong marriage?

_____

_____

Summary:

You can each take proactive steps to ensure a successful marriage. For example, you can commit to praying together, reading the Bible together, and attending church as a couple. Communication is key, and you can work on building trust, understanding, and empathy by practicing active listening, being vulnerable, and expressing gratitude. It is also important for couples to prioritize quality time together and pursue shared interests and hobbies. Committing to these positive habits and behaviors can lay a solid foundation for a strong, fulfilling Christian marriage.

Final Summary

You have done it! You have completed this marriage curriculum and are on your way to a lifelong, thriving marriage relationship. I am so happy you took the time to prepare for the most important relationship of your life. You will never regret the efforts you put into thoughtfully reading this material and asking yourselves some of these critical questions.

I am often asked by engaged and married couples alike if I could summarize the best path to a lasting, happy marriage. I believe three important topics must be addressed to maintain a solid marriage relationship. They are communication, intimacy, and money. If you will simply commit to talking about everything, be intimate with each other as often as possible, and manage your money wisely, you will make it! It is not that hard, but it does take commitment.

As you move forward to your wedding day, I encourage you to remain humble and honest with each other, striving to out-serve one another if possible, considering each other first, above anything or anyone else. In short, keep putting God first!

Trust GOD from the bottom of your heart;
do not try to figure out everything on your own.
Listen for GOD'S voice in everything you do,
He's the one who will keep you on track.
Proverbs 3:5-6 (MSG)

Notes:

_____

_____

_____

_____

_____

_____

_____

_____

_____

_____

_____

_____

_____

_____

_____

_____

_____

_____

_____

_____

_____

www.ingramcontent.com/pod-product-compliance
Lightning Source LLC
Chambersburg PA
CBHW042346030426
42335CB00031B/3479